Sowell
Collection
Books

THE LAST MAN
IN WILLAPA

AND OTHER POEMS

ROBERT MICHAEL PYLE

TEXAS TECH UNIVERSITY PRESS

This book is typeset in Adobe Caslon Pro. The paper used in this book meets the minimum requirements of ANSI/NISO Z39.48-1992 (R1997). ⊗

Designed by Hannah Gaskamp
Cover design by Hannah Gaskamp
Cover illustration by Neil Johannsen

Library of Congress Cataloging-in-Publication Data

Names: Pyle, Robert Michael, author. Title: The Last Man in Willapa: And Other Poems / Robert Michael Pyle. Description: Lubbock, Texas: Texas Tech University Press, 2024. | Series: Sowell Collection Books | Summary: "A collection of poems that explore the nature, large and small, of the physical world and the stories of its varied inhabitants"—Provided by publisher. Identifiers: LCCN 2023051126 | ISBN 978-1-68283-217-2 (cloth) Subjects: LCGFT: Poetry. Classification: LCC PS3616.Y545 L37 2024 | DDC 811/.6—dc23/ eng/20231101 LC record available at https://lccn.loc.gov/2023051126

Printed in the United States of America
24 25 26 27 28 29 30 31 32 / 9 8 7 6 5 4 3 2 1

Texas Tech University Press
Box 41037
Lubbock, Texas 79409-1037 USA
800.832.4042
ttup@ttu.edu
www.ttupress.org

For the Girl in the Yellow Towel

CONTENTS

Part I: Threnody

Part II: The Cuba Poems

Part III: The Children of the Night

Part IV: From the River

Part V: Ceremony

THE LAST MAN IN WILLAPA

PART 1

THRENODY

The Last Man in Willapa

Before, there were bears. Then there was
Weyerhaueser, Crown Zellerbach, and hounds.
The hound-hunters and timberbeasts wiped out
the black bears of Willapa, who had a taste
for sweet cambium of Douglas-fir. But when
the companies sold out and hounds were banned,
the bears came back.

More and more folks saw black bears in Willapa.
Birdfeeders went down. Rumors flew. The years
went by. Everyone was seeing bears. Everyone,
that is, except for him. He saw a puma, he saw bobcats.
He saw otters, mink, and muskrats. He even saw
that elusive rodent, the Aplodontia. But bears—
he couldn't spot one for the life of him.

Then one day the hired hand ran in and said
"I met a bear—a big one!" They found its splats
of wild honeycomb and pears. Next day,
the last man in Willapa to see a bear
saw the bear beside his mailbox,
waiting for delivery, or for him
for a change.

Threnody for a Fawn

Those tiny triangles of ears
could have been coyote's
poking up, there above
the center line. But no:
it's a fawn, no bigger than a pup.
Crows jumping out of the way
of every car that comes along
as baby buckskin melds with road
and white spots run together with the red.
What's the point, you want to cry,
of a life so little lived as this?

Last night, at twilight, a doe poked
her nose out of brush down the slope.
Beside her, spots congealed
from the shadows: a newborn fawn.
Another . . . and a third! Triplets,
on unsteady legs, ready
for what comes next,
fading back into the dusk.

Pantoum for the Common Mouse

Wee, sleekit, cow'rin, and tim'rous you may be
and cute as hell, for sure. But too prolific
by a long shot, and you know, you just crap
all over the house. The center cannot hold.

Cute as hell, for sure. But too prolific
for your own good, if you know what I mean.
All over the house, the center cannot hold,
so the traps must out, and I am not responsible.

For your own good, if you know what I mean,
because your species evolved to live outside.
So the traps must out, and I am not responsible.
Or so I like to think, as I free your shattered skull.

Because your species evolved to live outside,
your kin will surely be happier in the rotting rain
(or so I like to think, as I free your shattered skull)
than making a nest in my warm kitchen linens.

Your kin will surely be happier in the rotting rain
(cold and wet, but natural, don't you see?)
than making a nest in my warm kitchen linens,
sprinkling your little black turds all over, and dying.

Cold and wet, but natural, don't you see?
How much better for us both that would be, than
sprinkling your little black turds all over, and dying,
wee, sleekit, cow'rin, and tim'rous though you be.

Quoth the Fisherman

"Even if you die sometime," said the fisherman in the pub,
"You'd better be holdin' on to something."
Wait, what? "Even *if* you die," like it's a *question*?
Or is this the question: just what you'd best be clinging to
when the deal, or the boat, goes down.
Or maybe this: what if you *don't* die sometime—
do you still have to hold on?

The Day After the Election

(November 2016)

A red oak leaf and a brown beech leaf lie
across a wet sword fern frond in the late sun.
A chorus frog does a hoarse solo on the hill,
a flicker cries a series of sharp single notes.
The sun falls, the mist rises all over the valley.
These things at least, I guess,
will go on.

The Day After the Inauguration

(January 2017)

A pair of goldeneyes spin and dive
in a riffle below the covered bridge.
Hazel catkins swell and stretch,
not long till budburst. Back home,
chickadees have found the feeders
at last! Feared they weren't coming
at all this year—but here they are.

Nordic Noir

I've been reading Nordic Noir mysteries lately: *The Girl* this,
The Ice that. To someone of a boreal nature, such as I, death
and mayhem seem more at home on bleak Icelandic moors,
in sodden Swedish streets, than in some sunny southern clime.
But lately I think I've had enough for now. I want to read
about the cherry bloom in Jutland, lambing in the Lake District,
the Borealis bouncing off Beluga's snowy snout. There's just so much
noir in Noir! How much can one soul take
until it needs a breath of fresh air? Until it needs to look
right into the Midnight Sun?

Pretty in Pink

Old guys like me, our skin just isn't pretty.
It's been through the wars, after all these years
in the sun. It's a minefield—a *fertile* field,
for all kinds of lumps and moles and tags.
I went to the skin doc today, to see what harm
another year had done.

Last time, a pound of flesh from the face.
My back, my arms, my head—an archipelago
of keratoses, both actinic and seborrheic,
a shoal of freckles, bumps, and spots.
Maybe a basal cell cancer, maybe a squamous,
like the one that left my new Frankenstein scar.
Angiomas, lipomas, fibromas—just so she doesn't say
"melanoma," the one we never want to hear.

This time I got off easy: just 25 or 30 blasts
of liquid nitro, and not a scalpel to be seen. Plus,
the doc said my butt was a ten, and wrote it down!
And that I had a couple of pips on my shoulder,
whose medical name I'd never heard before:
"They're called *pearly pink papules*," she said.
Aha! Something pretty, after all.

Girl in Yellow Towel

He was frying eggs. She came
out of the bathroom to show him the pepper.
Turned to go, then turned back, and said
"Girl in Towel."
And so she was. Standing there glowing,
hair all curly damp, wrapped
in a bright yellow towel.
"Girl in Towel," he echoed.
Moved his hand from spatula
to moist, warm back. Pulled her closer,
she in her bright yellow towel,
the color of the yolks
clotting in the skillet.

Whiskey and Pie

The gods were duly invoked: Hugo, Kittredge. Duncan
was there, and Robert Lee, and a covey of godlets to be.
Whiskey was drunk, words spoken, cheers rendered,
200 pies consumed. Declined, this morning, good company
for a walk along the Clark Fork. Wanted it lonely, and quiet.

Footbridge, signs about the Missoula Floods, about
cleaning up Milltown, where Hugo used to drink.
Far enough along the Kim Williams Nature Trail, past
construction and kids on day release, most of the runners,
riders, walkers, left behind, all comes quiet. Hear only
river's cascades and kingfishers, chickarees and flicker,
one dee-dee-dee of a blackcap, one single syllable
of some migrant's warble, obligatory whistle of a train
heading up-canyon.

Coloring up, just after equinox: mountain ash berries'
bright burn, roan creek dogwood, broken-yolk box elder,
scarlet fingers and night-blue fruits of Virginia creeper.
Juniper juice on one forefinger and thumb, cottonwood
balsam on the other; sweet & bitter, yin & yang, absinthe & gin.
So many sensations, out here past town.

Hidden from path by cherry thicket, juniper
grows from base of old Douglas-fir, holding
its thick butt with its ropy roots. Fir sticks
out at the river till trunk straightens up, makes
flat lap, squirrel midden. Says "Sit here! Take
a load off. Write a poem or something." And who
am I to resist? Three female mergansers lie up
against a rock in the Clark Fork below.

Dinner at the Grange

A moose came to Grange tonight from Nova Scotia,
shot and roasted to perfection by Farmer Phil.
And mangos, rolled in coconut and chocolate,
brought by Amelia from Skamokawa.
Mike the County Commissioner stir-fried
leeks and zucchini and mushrooms.
Darbury made her famous pizza, Sulema
her chicken pie. Broccoli and pecan salad appeared,
and fresh sourdough bread. It's been years since Pies
for Polio went by the wayside, along with Jell-O,
and our-long-running oyster stew night is history too,
along with Norman Anderson, who made it.
But though the menu evolves with the membership,
we eat well here at Grange.
The hunters and the vegans,
the bakers and gardeners and fishers,
the R's and D's, longhairs and short,
we Patrons of Husbandry break bread together
and burp.

Bigfoot Poem

Professors who have the time of day for Bigfoot are few
and far between. There was Professor Holm, UW, told me in '69
that every Indian he knew, still of land and water, had no doubt
that Dzonoqua walks, just like bear and beaver; thinks us silly to ask.
And Professor Krantz, WSU, Keeper of the Open Mind
and greatest horde of footprint casts and tracks. He broke trail,
took academic hell for it. "I don't *believe*," he said. "I *accept*—
on the evidence." Called it *Gigantipithecus canadensis*.
Next came Professor Meldrum, Idaho State U. Named a mob of proto-
hominids new to science, and one fossil species based on footprints,
the very ape of whom we speak: *Anthropoidipes ameriborealis*.
Before all of them was Professor Napier, Head of Primatology,
Smithsonian. Concluded either Bigfoot was real, which he thought
ridiculous; or else a hoax of such elegance as to be impossible.
Came to prefer the ridiculous over the impossible. And
Professor Goodall, of Gombe Forest. Considering my book,
she asked, "Why are you so circumspect? The evidence,"
she told me, "is overwhelming."
So what about you, Professor Pyle? What do you believe?
I'm not sure, having seen only one, in the dusk. But those sounds . . .
those tracks. I have no better explanation. I await word from the final
source. But Bigfeet who have the time of day for professors are few
and far between.

What If We Had a Poet for President?

(2018)

We had a well-published one, you know, in Jimmy Carter.
Washington, Adams, Lincoln, and Obama also wrote verse in office.
We could have had a good one in Gene McCarthy, Chicago, '68—
then the war would have ended five years before it did,
there would have been no Watergate, and who knows what else?

Poets have seldom called the shots. Nezahualcóyotl was poet
and ruler of Texcoco in Mexico, but his verses did not prevent
the Spanish conquest of the Aztec Empire. Look where his odes got Neruda,
and his boss, Allende: prosody being no match for the CIA.

Even so, imagine how humane ideals might reign
with Whitman in the White House. Or how hope
and wild geese might thrive on a Dickinson-Oliver ticket.
How the world might make sense, if Snyder ruled the roost.

But what do we get instead?
The inarticulate dregs of an incurious mind,
the bottom of the barrel,
one hundred and forty characters deep.

Outside the Phoenix Inn

(Eugene, early March)

Red maple flowers,
white camellias, yellow
daffodils. A ripple against
a rock in the bed of the old canal
below my window.
Steller's jay clatters past,
junco scuffles under curly willow.
Details such as these,
and the nippy breeze through
the window screen,
make a motel stay
a field trip.

Man Hit Twice by Train

Train #14, northbound, four hours late
already, thanks to the freights on the line.
Late afternoon, rolling into Portland.
Some passengers feel a slight bump,
train stops fast. We sit and sit.
Conductor walks through, apologizes
for further delay, closes curtains on the right side.
No one says it, but all the police cars and lights,
yellow tape, ambulance, the stretcher, make it clear:
someone's been hit. Another hour off the clock,
and no one complains. Much later, the news explains:
"Man between tracks struck by two trains."
First the up-train passenger got him, then,
for Christ's sake, the down-bound freight.
Sometimes lightning does strike twice,
zapping the same unlucky person. But
how the hell do you get slammed by two trains?
And by what dumb luck is that man still alive?

Hazels

They're the first flowers of spring,
both the wild hazel-nuts and the filberts.
Only halfway into January,
and here they are: up and down
the Willamette Valley and points north,
their long golden danglers hanging—
catkins casting pollen
on waning winter's winds.
Older orchards spread gilded clouds
over hill and dale, new ones glow
in rows of little yellow globes.
From stark winter woods of maple, fir, and alder
peers the pale presence of wild hazel,
late Christmas trees strung with brassy tinsel.
Well before the first snowdrops and crocus
it is the hazels—or filberts, if you prefer—
that promise we'll make it through, once more.

Shims

On the southbound *Coast Starlight*, needing a good night's sleep,
I have splurged on a sleeper. René, the friendly attendant
for the sleeping cars, folds down the cot in my roomette
and I climb into it, ready to be rolled
into sweet slumber.
But wait—there's a rattle! That won't do.
The door of my compartment clatters with every sway
and curve. But not to worry, it's easy to fix. I fold
a safety card, jam it into the gap, lock the door tight.
This quiets the ride, and I sleep like a babe, sweet dreams
to the lullaby of the singing rails and tales of distant lights.

What I have made is called a shim. Do you suppose
the word comes from "shimmy"? Because that's what it stops.
Anyway, it makes me think: isn't a shim a kind of a wedge?
And yet wedges drive things apart, while shims nudge
them closer, level them out, stop the rattle, roll, and pitch.
I wonder whether that might be what kills many loves,
when what they need is just a little shim now and then;
but what they make instead is a big, fat wedge.

Going Viral: A Plague in Three Acts

I. Going Viral

takes on a whole new meaning these days,
having to do with *actual germs*—as opposed
to the usual sense of pup and kitty pictures zooming
around the world at light speed on particles that infect
many a mind with way too little to do, while leaving
the body itself, and the soul, almost untouched.

II. Blowing Kisses

When Márquez wrote *Love in the Time of Cholera*
little did he imagine the sequel that would write itself today
in Facetime, dating apps, waves through the windows of ICUs,
blowing kisses from at least six feet: *Love in the Time of Corona.*
If, as biologists say, the problem with pandemic is population,
then this could help! Keeping our distance from everyone else—
what better form of birth control? But wait . . . the ones
locked down together will be coupling like bunnies!
It's a dumb germ that doesn't look to its future.

III. Corvids 19

As shadows grow toward the end of this tender April day
one scrub jay scrawls from the valley below. Its deep blue
cousin, the Steller's, trades lowlands for the hills about now,
but three still make a night-blue racket at the feeder.
Crows stream downriver each dawn, dawdle back up
in the evening. A baker's dozen caw and rattle here now.
While overhead, the happiest of lovers, pair of ravens,
gliding, clucking, smug. So that's the score at my place
today: hummingbirds 2, corvids 19. It won't make CNN.

The New Normal

Blood-red moonglade on Snoqualmie River.
Blood-red half-moon going down, upstream.
Red Saturn riding a black skyline of firs,
redder than Mars ever thought of being.
Red moonglade, red moon, red Saturn:
Forest fires.
Red eyes!
But that moonglade,
like hammered copper in midstream—
that was beautiful.

Certainties

On a winter's day, eight freighters lie at anchor
off the Oregon side. Their white bridges and red hulls,
all in a line, catch the late sun, shimmer against misty hills
across the river. From the shoreline, purple forest runs
up into sky a paler blue than any eggshell.
Plimsoll lines parallel the surface, calm as it ever gets,
colder than the crews ever know in Singapore, Taipei, Luzon.

As lights come on in the rigging, the sun fizzles into the bar,
and the girl in the panda cap rises from her bench to go, I know
three things. This moment will never come again. The river
(as they say and say, and say again) will never be the same river.
And this can of ale—no matter how I nurse it—
will run out.

It is good to have some certainties in life.

PART II

THE CUBA

POEMS

Abandoned in Havana

Nothing since that empanada at the airport
but a couple of beers. So when seven o'clock comes
and nobody shows up for dinner, I step out
to forage on my own. Cuba is new,
my Spanish sucks, and I am none too sure.
But somehow I find the porch of El Presidente,
a Carib fish filet, an Argentinian Carménère,
as the old Dodges and DeSotos rumble past
and the pretty women blow by on the cool breeze
in the palms. A young man places a helmet
on his girlfriend's head, they mount a motorbike.
Kids gather on the sidewalk for the hotel's wi-fi.
Fidel was buried yesterday, so after nine days of silence
the music starts again tonight. Down the veranda
a four-woman band—singer in white, plus maracas,
congas, electric bass, and acoustic flute—blazes
through a tight Cubana set. A shot of Cuban rum
has landed in my hand. I guess I'll make it
through my abandonment, after all.

On the Malecón

After the day, after a nap, after rum at sunset, I walk
down to the Bay, the long seawall called the Malecón. Turn
south toward the river. Along the Malecón lovers caress,
runners sweat, yogis stretch. Fishermen cast out, some with poles,
some just spools. A boy shows me the sea-perch he's just pulled in.
Waves slap over coral to the seawall on my right, make
the sidewalk green and slick with algae. Fumes slap
from the other side, sea of traffic where schools of green
'54 Fords and blue '49 Chevies tool the broad four-lane.
Busking *guitarreros* and prostitutes troll for customers,
languid boys with cell phones, girls arm-in-arm in short shorts
and bright skirts. A plastic bag, blown up with sea breeze,
races me all along the Malecón to the Rio Almendares.

Off the Malecón

The dark neighborhoods are quiet but
for soft voices of children in the streets.
Doors open, bare-chested men before TVs,
women talking like soft birds in the night.
In a little corner bakery I buy a sticky bun
for a peso. A black woman buying bread says
"You should stay here in Havana!" and
the white baker nods his agreement. "Here,"
she says, "there is no color."

The Cats of Havana

are black and white. Okay, a few gingers and tabbies,
a calico or two. But on the whole, black and white. Also
many are polydactyl, like Hemingway's cats in Key West.

It is said the cats of Cuba disappeared into cooking pots
after the collapse of the Soviet Union, when hunger hit
the country hard. But now they're back. It is said

that all sorts of changes are coming, now that the U.S.A.
is back too. Will *yanqui* dollars improve lives here?
Or just make the rich richer? Will this invasion work,
where the Bay of Pigs failed? Everyone wonders
what's to come.

Meanwhile, the cats of Havana carry on
their nightly prowl.

The Bats of Havana

whisk past my shoulder
leaving echoes
of ink and gauze.

The Tour

David takes me on a long and arduous walk
through the streets of Central to the Old Town.
On the way, the university. A young man approaches,
tells us he is Iván, a student. Leads us on a tour
through backstreets. "Here is Fidel's house as a student!"
"Here is the bar where Fidel and Che plotted and drank—
at that very table!" "We should drink here too!" So we do—
to the *Revolucionarias*, to us, to *Cuba y USA*—on us.
Afterward David tells me that Iván was no student,
and we were taken for a ride. Those shrines? Who knows.
No matter. I've been taken for worse of a fool
before. It was cheap, an experience, a story to tell,
and Iván ate well that night. Later, our friends recount
meeting two professors at the university,
who took them on a tour . . .

Sitting in Fidel's Study Carrel

in Antonio Núñez Jiménez Foundation for Man and Nature.
Núñez Jiménez, the great geographer, fought with Che,
had Fidel's lifelong friendship. These eight carrels came
from Castro's old college. Pink silk upholstered chairs,
glass-topped, brass-lit, slanted mahogany writing desks.
Theses, manuscripts, and books fill tall shelves all 'round.
Soft murmurs of scholars and poets through sliding doors.
How I would love to write more than these few lines here.
Oh! WHAT I would write here!

Among the Writers

Cuban and American writers sit down together
in two facing rows of square tables, each a display
case of fossils, formations, minerals, medals,
regalia, and souvenirs of *La Revolución*. Tall shelves
hold Núñez Jiménez's manuscripts on one side,
his bound books of photographs on the other.
Che, Fidel, and their comrades-in-arms peer
from framed black-and-white pictures on both walls.
We take turns reading our poems and papers up front.
Armando MCs, comments on each one, the way they do
here. The poems go mostly in their own language,
taken for their rhythm and flow. Luis translates lucidly, but
a long paper on gender in Cuban fairy tales is a challenge.
To be honest, we all find it a challenge, in either language.
But then, from between all the lines of arid scholarship,
comes this:
  "I used to live in a pumpkin, inside a pumpkin patch."
And this:
           "Make your baskets,
     fill them up with butterflies and fireflies,
    wait for me, and we will make a good party."
And, frankly? I would have come to Cuba just for that.

At the Writers' Union

(La Unión de Escritores y Artistas de Cuba)

We *yanqui* poets and scholars are invited
to a reception for a famous photographer,
a rare honor for outsiders. Our gifts of books
for the library are received without fanfare.

After the honoree speaks, wine is served. Look
around for someone I can speak with, pounce
on the owner of the only voice I savvy.
Leonardo, professor of English, is here
with his niece Yurisan and nephew Evelio.
Leonardo strongly resembles Barack Obama.
"Did you suffer any cases of mistaken identity," I ask,
"during the president's recent visit to Cuba?" "Only
once," he says. "It was the Belgian Ambassador."

In the Botanic Garden

(La Quinta de los Molinos)

On the bus to *La Quinta de los Molinos*, Luis talks
about the Rolling Stones. Their free concert
in Havana, he says, was the highlight of his life
so far. I tell him about Seattle in '94 and '05.
But now we are here. Marisela and Danielle guide
us through the Eco-Park, show us Bahaman swallowtails,
monarchs, and zebras in the *Mariposario*. Outside,
rusty bumblebees visit lilies, scarlet dragonflies skim
the koi pond, red-legged thrushes work the greenery.

When the rest leave for a hot walk through Havana Vieja,
I stay behind where gulf fritillaries and Baracoa skippers
haunt weedy corners. Later, forage for lunch in smoky streets,
smuggle two baby bananas and a beer back into the garden.
On a bench beneath a bower, a nest above my head, cooled
by a breeze off the dragonfly pond, two more hours to explore
this oasis in the teeming city before I catch an old car back—
in this place of notorious poverty, why do I feel so rich?

PART III

THE CHILDREN
OF THE NIGHT

1. The Children of the Night Went Forth

The children of the night went forth
into the soft evenings of suburbia.
As soon as they could open the screen door
the dimity drew them forth
and there was no one to say no
because that's what children did
in those days, in that place, where
dusk and freedom wore the same clothes
and had the same unspoken name.

2. The Children of the Night Await Their Dad

When late afternoons were warm and waiting
to turn into twilight, the children sat in their
front yard to await their father's return from work.
All the other dads were filing home too in Chevies,
Fords, and Dodges. As each one wheeled slowly past,
the children waved and giggled and shouted
"Hi my dad-dy!" to each puzzled pa. But they
were watching for the Packard, which finally arrived,
with *their* daddy, and his Lucky Strike hug.

3. The Children of the Night Make Christmas Plans

In the winter they seldom went forth after dark, except
to rescue the paper from the snow before it got too wet
to read. Leading up to Christmas, panels of "Rudolph"
appeared on the front page, with red ink. They waited
to read it with their dad before he dove into the paper,
their mom into the kitchen to make dinner. And when
dark fell, because bedtime was early and the night
was cold, they dove under the covers and made plans
for Christmas, which were always the same.

4. The Children of the Night Go Forth by Day

"Who are we that we should walk in the night . . ."
—John Russell McCarthy, *For the Morning*

When they awoke to the chink of Cheerios in the bowl
and the sun shone through the iris-scented screen
the children of the night became the children of the day.
Then they rose, stretched their scrawny backs, donned
the garb of ordinary boys, attacked their cereal and toast,
and headed outside . . . to the backyard? The park?
Or the longer walk to the endless wild ditch,
where smells and rills from distant meltings made
the day almost as seductive as the night?

5. The Children of the Night Try to Puncture the Sky

"or try to be friends with the strange cold gods of the skies . . ."
—John Russell McCarthy, *For the Morning*

There were afternoons those summers that
hung so dark and lowering that the sky itself
might as well have been lead, as lightning
and the promise of rain hung like love-notes
in the West, never posted. That's when they sharpened
handfuls of #3 pencils and *flung*
them into the thick air over their heads, hoping
to pierce the heavy bellies of the lowest clouds,
releasing the rain that would solve everything.

6. Are the Children of the Night Ever Incubi and Succubi?

Some might wonder, the way they came and went
throughout the house, in and out of any bed.
Who'd blame them for thinking the worst?
In a different story, a darker time, possessions
happen. In a different story in different hands,
diabolical things might befall, no one the wiser.
But these children were too young, too innocent,
and didn't know those tales. Their visitations
were solely for love, and warmth, and comfort.

7. The Children of the Night Fly Kites

Every March there came a day when the wind was up
and everyone stormed the drugstore to buy new kites.
The dads donned gray sweatshirts or flannels to help
the children put them together. One always chose
a black & red man in the moon; the other, Saturn
and its rings in yellow and blue. Then the whole block
came out and put their kites to the sky. Their dad let
them hold the strings, hoping they wouldn't let go for
once, just to watch him chase it all down the street.

8. The Children of the Night Play Hide and Seek

Then came summer. And with it, dusks like velvet
in their warmth and softy dark. Everyone came outside,
but no dads or moms—just the kids. No sooner
did they emerge into the night (their natural habitat)
and meet to check in and set rules, than they dispersed
to bush, shed, cranny, shadow, and hid. From there
it was only an assumption they would ever be found.
Yet somehow, knowing for sure they'd be back again
tomorrow night, they all made it home for supper.

9. The Children of the Night Hold Dog Day

When the family had spare ribs for dinner, they
took care to leave meat on the bone, and saved
all the gnawed ribs in a brown shopping bag.
Then they slipped out the back screen door, down
the lawn, over the fence and into the alleys—a secret
network behind the houses, alternate routes for kids
and other animals. At every yard with a dog,
they flung the ribs over the fence, crying
"Dog Day! Dog Day!" all through the neighborhood.

10. The Children of the Night Become Cat Man

On certain still evenings after sunset
the children took again to the alleyways,
now as the Night Raiders, no sack of bones
in hand. They took care to move quietly,
not to disturb the dogs with false hopes.
Slipped around houses, through the bushes,
paused with a silent nod. Then one of them
would *ululate* shrilly into the night,
and that's how they got to be Cat Man.

11. The Children of the Night Go to the Shopping Center

When the shopette rose from the cottonwood swamp,
they had a new place to haunt. One pushed the other
up and down the aisles in Busley's, calling "Frozen boy
for sale, frozen boy," until closing. Or they stuffed
the raffle barrel, and won the bike. But they did
no real harm. So when the dads butchered their deer
and hung them in the parking lot for all to admire,
the children could be forgiven, couldn't they,
for kyping some of the ribs for the dogs?

12. The Children of the Night Catch Moths

Some came to spring lilacs after rain in the dusk,
pink-winged sphinxes with hummingbird tongues.
Others clung to streetlight poles or the windowsills
of stores—scarlet, black, and cheddar tigers, scads
of army cutworms. But for the best specimens
(dove-gray *Tolype*, jade-green *Campaea*) they went
porch-light to porch-light in their neighborhood.
Nobody missed the moths they stole, and they were only
kids, so no guns, and only once did the sheriff show up.

13. The Children of the Night Visit the Witch

The old red house just had to have a witch.
Sometimes they saw her watering lilacs where
swallowtails loitered, but that didn't fool them.
So one night they dared their way onto her veranda,
where millers battered the screen by the hundreds.
How they jumped when the back door screeched
and she appeared. "Take all you want of those,"
she said, waving at the moths. It ended with cookies
and lemonade, and her name was Robina.

14. The Children of the Night Sell Stuff

Whoever condemned child labor did not know
the Children of the Night. Lazy as a rule, they could
work their little butts off to make a nickel. Dig peach-
cans of dandelions, cut lawns, wash cars. But best,
for spawn of a salesman, was selling stuff. Kool-Aid,
of course, from a card table, but also door-to-door:
White Cloverine Salve, Burpee Seeds, Christmas cards,
even seashells: "Jewels of the sea!" they'd call.
Customers saw them coming and locked their doors.

15. The Children of the Night Do Halloween

One always went as a tiger, the other as a leopard.
Or a knight in armor and a desperado, according
to their reigning passions. Their mom dressed
the hall lamp as a witch to scare the trickers,
but mostly scared the tiger, giving him nightmares
on his sugar-filled stomach. Each year, they enjoyed
their one sanctioned venture deep into the night—
neighbor to neighbor, claiming *bags* of candy
as tribute from those who never bought their salve.

16. The Children of the Night Scare Howard

The children were not always nice, such as
the night of the underground chicken house.
One took Howard into the culvert under Del Mar
to hide from the other, as someone (or some *thing*?)
crept toward them under a streetlight, flapping
like some great bat. When it howled into the tunnel,
Howard screamed and peed his pants.
And the abandoned underground chicken house?
Well, that part doesn't bear speaking about.

17. The Children of the Night Cruise the Hinterlands

On bikes, they sped down the ditchrider's road
along the old canal at sunset. Took farm roads east
and north, into the darkness at the edge of town,
watched for pronghorns, dodged tumbleweeds.
When summer rain hit ripe winter wheat in late
slant sun it loosed a sweet and dangerous smell
that entered by the nose, then struck them *smack*
in their budding gonads, sending them into spasms
and dreams for which they had no name.

18. The Children of the Night Listen to Rock 'n' Roll

The old box radio they inherited for their room
when the house got hi-fi was impartial. It played
everything democratically—Pogo Poge the Weird
Beard from KIMN to Wolfman Jack, 250,000 watts
out of the Mexican pirate radio. Songs of love,
songs of loss, songs of break-ups and make-ups;
Annette & Bobby & Connie & Fabian & all the rest,
setting their own myths in motion, fairy tales they'd
never get over, and all they had to do was dream.

19. The Children of the Night Get Cars

When their dad brought the Cushman home from work
their bikes gave way to scooters. But their Vespas went
only so far—the mountains, the state line—and it's hard
to make out on a motor scooter. So when they hit sixteen
they bought old Fords for next to nothing. Drivers' Ed
got them out of class and out of the city limits, but
it was Friday nights that took them out of their minds,
to cottonwood grove, copse, and Antelope Hill. And that,
as they say, was all she wrote.

20. Twilight of the Children of the Night

And now, when they enter the dusky airs,
the children only think they remember
what it was like and what it was all about
and how it smelled, and how it felt, when
pint-sized versions of their gangly selves *strode*
into the twilights of yore. Days and nights galore
yawned before them, or so it seemed back then.
But now, somehow, the nights have no names,
only numbers.

21. The Children of the Night
Go Forth No More

One by one, they come into their majority, and leave
the things of childhood behind. No more dog days, no
more pencils hurled to the sky. No more the night! For
now they have jobs, and mates, and they spend the dark
hours indoors more often than not, or looking down
when they go out. And then come young of their own.
But the nights are no longer hospitable to children, or
so they are deemed by those who once had the run
of the lovely evenings, but deny it now to their darlings.

And the night, the night—
it wonders where the children have gone.
It misses them.

PART IV

FROM THE
RIVER

The Book Boat

He bought a good old tub named *Lorraine*
off an old salt gone to shore on Sauvie Island.
Barely knew navigation, let alone diesel,
so come spring and still afloat, he found a mate—
a worse-off soak, never dried out, in a tavern
off lower Burnside on Water Street—
to caulk decks, pump bilge, romance
the fickle engine into life.

When it began to look like *Lorraine* might not sink,
he built shelves in the hold, and started buying
books wherever he could: Goodwills and thrifts
in The Dalles and St. Helens, library sales in Rainier
and White Salmon, the remainder tables at Powell's.
Then, recalling bookmobiles from his boyhood
on the plains, he hung his shingle on the bridge,
and took The Book Boat on the road—on the river.

And so it went, up and down the tidal reach,
Bonneville to Baker Bay and back again.
Sometimes through the locks, all the way
to Lewiston. Laying his wares before the boaters,
the fishers, the workers, the loafers, all of them
hungry for good books, though they might not know it.
He sold them cheap, gave them away, or—
his favorite—bartered, for fish, fruit, or laundry.
Swapped a late Brian Doyle for a sturgeon,
Middlemarch for Maryhill wine. Made enough
for ground beef, beer, and diesel. Even the cat got fed,
and the mate paid enough for drunken leave ashore.
Lorraine became a legend, up and down the river.
Marinas vied for her, gave free moorage for a night
or three. Until he started to wonder about the islands,
the Inside Passage, and beyond. So he took *Lorraine*
across the bar, and didn't die. Put in at LaPush,

where he sold all of his Pushkin to a Russian emigré,
and a set of *Twilight* to a wannabe werewolf. Then east
up the Straits: Neah Bay, Sekiu, P.A., P.T.,
and Points North. Last rumors came from Kodiak.
But even now the Columbia remembers. And there's
always a slip open, just in case.

Cottonwoods in March

(Willow Grove)

After the dance, you drove out Willow Grove,
across the bridge beyond the town,
between river and backwater slough.
The warm night beguiled by cottonwoods
all along the bank, just breaking bud,
just putting out their soft green tongues,
all sticky with the brown paste of balsam,
once called Balm of Gilead. Both of you
taken by the cloying scent
far beyond sense. You knew you shouldn't park,
but you did. And stroked
each other's faces
with the soft green spears
(cheeks, eyelids, right below the greedy nostrils,
lips), lacerating your hearts beyond repair.
A pleasure so intense (the two senses least used,
smell and touch) that you could never, ever,
speak it as it was.
Barely even kissed. But you both knew—
didn't you?—that the kisses would come,
and you could only hope
they would match the sweetness
of those cottonwood strokes
on Willow Grove
that night.

Rooster Rock Blues

How dare a basalt thumb stick up like that?
But not a thumb—obviously had a different, rhyming name
to sailors, sanitized later for delicate state park goers.
Like a similar protrusion in Utah, sandstone not lava,
bowdlerized into the Bishop's Finger. Funnily enough,
Rooster Rock became the site of sanctioned public nudity—
first official clothing-optional beach on the river. Now,
when summer-evening volleyball takes place,
all those so-called "roosters" flop like headless chickens,
up and down along the sandy shore, together
with breasts and bellies and ponytails. Bouncy bouncy,
all captives of gravity, all unchained melodies. Meanwhile
in thickets of red osier dogwood above the beach,
echo azure butterflies dance and mate—Frost's
"sky flakes down in flurry on flurry." Females tucking
their eggs like tiny rounds of cheese
in between the carpels of coming waves
of creamy blooms, where their babies will graze, *insensible*
to all the merely human goings-on
in the lengthening shadow of Rooster Rock.

Old Gold, She Said

It was time to go.
They'd made a good try.
All along the river,
dreams have come and gone.
Dreams lie broken like
crawdad shells around
a summer pond. Just that,
again. The banks of the tribs
are studded with gray wood
hulks and rusted frames
of old cars where the water rose
and the people left. They might
have made good life together
till then. Sometimes the water
rising wasn't water, but life
itself. Anyway, it was time.
They weren't some of those
for whom it all worked out
in the long run. So they drove
east on the 4, toward the 5,
the city, and what came next.

The cottonwoods,
oaks, and ashes arrayed
along the backwaters held on
to the last rich color of the fall.
"It looks like old gold," she said.
And he almost wondered . . .
but it was time to go.

Them Dams

Them dams, them dams, them crazy dams,
each one choking up the river's throat
like a swollen glottis, call them glottal stops
for the flow, the fish, the whole blessed channel.
Killing off salmon like God's own gaff,
wiping out cultures like the cavalry charging
down from Calvary on high. Roll on Columbia,
Celilo Falls and all the rest can just be go to hell.

That's one of the things I like best
about the tidewater reach of the river:
all the way from Bonneville
on down to the bar,
as far as you look—
there ain't *no damn dams.*

River of Carbon

for Columbia Riverkeeper

At this late stage,
late in the day of the carnival of carbon
there are still those who want to reduce this river
to a conduit for fossil fuels.
Liquefied natural gas at Bradwood.
Giant coal terminal plus massive
methane plant at Kalama.
Oil dump for igneous trains in Vancouver.
All to fuel the carbon hungers
of China and the rest of the catch-up world
beyond the river's mouth. Never mind
all the life in the river
or the people who dwell along its banks.

But they forgot about those people
and how they might not like it,
and what they just might do about it.
And so they went down, one by one:
R.I.P., LNG; Bon Voyage, coal depot.

Don't mind us. It's just that we prefer
a River of H_2O.

Ghosts of Trojan

When I look out now from Cathlamet's shore
to Puget Island and see twin silos poking up
from a disused dairy farm, I think of the outsize tower
dominating downstream, past Rainier, for thirty years:
relic of that optimistic time when nuclear was expected
to be too cheap to meter.

Then came the arrests, the bumper stickers playing
on Trojan's name and shape, the cracks in steam pipes.
And finally the implosion, that squat prong collapsing
like a deliquescing mushroom, or a bull's spent part,
leaving the river a little radioactive, once again overseen
by silos having nothing to do with fission. You can see
them, looking out from Cathlamet's shore, poking up yet.

R.I.P., LNG

Talk about a way to wreck a river!
But they didn't count
on the people of the river,
and how they had no intention
of rolling over after all.

Liquefied Natural Gas:
a militarized river, closed
to ordinary traffic whenever
the bloated target came to town,
floating bomb beneath the bridge.

It was a long and bitter battle.
And when the bad actors
finally blew town, trailing
broken promises, debts, and bad odor
behind them,

among the papers in abandoned
files was found a top-secret list:
the order of incineration
of homes and properties,
in case of accident.

There will be no accident now,
no subjection of our river
to the captains of industry,
the masters of gas and cash.
Tenasillahee remains free!

R.I.P., LNG—
may we never see your like again,
or any other such ill-begotten plot.
And all those who put you in the ground?
Talk about a way to save a river!

I Cross the Columbia

How many times have I crossed this river?
Five hundred? A thousand? First time,
1964, with my mother, bringing me by rail
from Colorado to see her beloved Northwest.
It took. So there were many crossings to come
on the *Portland Rose*, the *City of Portland*, and
eventually Amtrak, or sometimes Greyhound,
Seattle to Denver and back again. Later,
in a dynasty of Volkswagens, it was I-5 and 205,
the Bridge of the Gods, Hood River, The Dalles,
Biggs, Umatilla, Vernita, and Vantage: for jobs,
field trips, family, all the reasons one has
for changing states of being. When I moved
downstream to a lower trib, crossings shifted
to the Lewis & Clark in Longview, the ferry
at Westport, in Honda, Toyota, Subaru.
Now I cross the river more than ever before—
at Megler, the last bridge before the bar.
And gladly so! For when I cross the Columbia now,
I am crossing it to you.

I Cover the Waterfront

(Ilwaco, December 2018)

Sometimes it seems the hopes of all mankind lie
on display in a small-town bookstore, against
all odds still open on a bleak December dock
in a time when so much else is going, going, gone.

After the reading I spill out the back door
onto the wet green waterfront. Walk
up and down in the dripping dusk. The slips
still have boats, though the fleet is tiny now.

Still, a good seafood grill, a pub, and Jessie's
Fish Market at the end of the pier persist.
I remember charters by the dozen, the cafe
at the end of the spit, Doupe's Hardware

as a going concern. But now it's mostly a matter
of the riverfront, where the Columbia brushes
Baker Bay before dying, or being born anew,
into the Ocean itself. And what moves me

is not what's gone, but what somehow remains:
the boats, the oysters, the books shiny in the light
through the wet window. They speak to the possibility
of all things, even in these times, waterfronts do.

As long as little seaside towns live on, giving harbor
to half-forgotten craft and vagabonds on a winter's night,
I will continue to cover the waterfront, seeking something
not likely to be found anywhere else.

PART V

CEREMONY

Ceremony

The roadkill was black, long, red at one end—a vulture?
Went back to look. My god, it's a bear! A tiny bear, tumped
up against the guard rail. Eighteen inches, maybe ten pounds
tops. Smaller than my cat, certainly skinnier. A tiny teddy:
head crushed, that's why the red. Sad, shocked, toss
him into the brush. Better, anyway, than hard asphalt.

But it doesn't sit right, like I haven't done right by the bear.
Some ceremony? A better, softer resting place? Go back today.
Heavy, brambly scramble down steep slope through cans
and plastic, ferns and firs, rotting branches. Hang onto sword fern
with its napthalene smell, hang over punji stakes of alder slash,
back and forth across that no-man's land between highway and life.
No sign; guess the coyotes took him already. Then, down final slope,
the bear—shiny fur, like acrylic in the sun, hung up in salal.

So I lift him—he's a little boy—by a paw. Less than a bag of sugar.
Farther down, mossy maple sticks out toward river. Teddies belong
on beds, says the little boy in me. Cinch way out the broad trunk, lay
little bear on his tummy on the bole. Stuff his busted jaw back in,
close his mouth with moss, lay paw over rubbery snout, the way my cat
likes to sleep. Feel those long, half-circle claws, thick and sharp;
those soft, cool pads like an old man's feet wrinkled by the rain.
Run my fingers through the soft fur that clothes that baby's body,
dry now, silky, warm in the evening sun.

Then clamber back up to the road, and down again, with four
long wands of false Solomon's seal, fragrant as orange blossom.
Squinch out the trunk again to lay the creamy racemes
around that shattered little head, you'd never know.
Say some words for the bear; for the world. Tug once more
his velvet elfin ears, turn, jump down, and go. Feel better now.

But later, over wine, I have to ask: who was it all for?
Some spirit bear? I don't think so. For the little bear?

A bear is just a bear, and the bear didn't care. Raven
watched the proceedings, and tomorrow the vultures will visit,
flowers scatter, little bear go back. So again I ask, who was it for?

For whom did I play "The Ballad of Frankie Lee and Judas Priest"
at my brother's funeral, lay new cottonwood shoots on his beautiful
cottonwood box? And for whom did I wash my own love's body,
dress her in soft white cotton, and flowers?

Easter Morning on the River Cam

Midsummer Common in the cool blue dawning
of the hottest Easter on record in the U.K.
Narrow boats moored with their flower pots
and some with solar panels. English robins,
wrens, chaffinches, and tits call and sing
in the plane trees, willows, and limes.

Then, here she comes:
a Cambridge lass in a single shell
sculling eastward, downstream.
Wearing a pale mauve jersey
and pink bunny ears
and leaving behind in her delicate wake
the perfect flicks from the tips of her oars

and a deep and permanent dent
in every heart that saw her
this Easter morning
on the River Cam.

Cheap as Chips

In a country renowned for its throne
you'd think they'd make a better toilet seat.
Thomas Crapper built a better toilet in 1880,
and things have gone downhill ever since.
Visiting my friend in Northamptonshire,
placing my fat but hardly massive ass
on the white plastic loo, I *winced*
at the sharp report when it broke in half.
How embarrassing! To have to report
to mine hosts that I'd cracked their pot,
just by perching, where their own sweet keisters
have perched a thousand times before, without incident.
But my friend unbarbed my shame
with elegance and thrift:
"Not to worry," said Nigel. "They're cheap as chips."
And really, is there anything good—
that Harris Tweed cap, the front and center seat
at Stratford, a good oak toilet seat—
if they serve the purpose and we love them—
of which we ought not say
not to worry—they're cheap as chips?
Because life is short, it's only money,
and you can't take it with you.

Breakfast with My Editor

We don't rise early. Breakfast often means noon.
I cut the fruit and bread while you do the eggs,
or vice versa, if we're boiling.
My opening gambit is likely to be a dream. Yours,
maybe an item in the news. Then we begin in earnest.
"Did you mean to say so and so?" you might ask,
not that it's a question. Or, "You were waiting *on* her,
were you? Wish I had someone waiting on me." Or
"Did you pick that expression up in England?" or
"Do they say that in Colorado?"
But the capper, when I go on and on about something,
is a jaunty "Ha ha! You think I'm listening!" from you.

Breakfast with my editor. Oh, what a lesson you are,
my sweet reviser, in concision, precision—
and incision: conversation by a thousand cuts.
I suppose it will go on this way.
I will be the better for it
and you, the dearer.

The Docs

We take ourselves unto them
over and over again. Put *our* selves
into *their* hands so they may feel us
and prod us, measure and weigh us,
probe us and prick us and shoot us
full of potions and rays and particles.
So they can cut us and slice us
and sew us back up, all
in the name of this little growth,
that big dis-ease, the aches,
breaks, quakes, and shakes,
whatever ailment encumbers
our bodies impolitic now.

Oh, for a box we could just step inside,
pull down the lid, turn on the switch,
then catch a few z's, chase a few dreams,
and *wake*—all well, all well, all . . .

well,
that's not going to happen.
So back we go, from appointment
to consult to "have a seat, the doctor
will be right with you."

Oh, the docs, the docs, the docs—
where would they be without us?

The Meadow

Beside a tiny lane in Worcestershire, painted Romany wagon camped nearby—
yes, there are a few around yet—beautiful paint horse grazing the lush verge.
But, that meadow: a national nature reserve, though it's just thirty acres. Well,
I was stunned. From hedgerow to forest, on all sides, this April-green sward
stretched out, *pelted* with a lemon-yellow density of cowslips, there must have been
millions. Among them, almost as thick, purple spotted and green-winged orchids:
each one a fairy's prom corsage. Not enough? Scattered
over that rich turf, deep patches and swaths of bluebells,
their scent as strong as the sight. I had to lean back against an oak.

All this richness here thanks to ancient farming: medieval tillage, grazing
and haying on careful schedule ever since, and never a chemical. Such
orchid-and-butterfly-rich grasslands common across England for centuries, irrigated
by English blood in the Wars of the Roses, the Civil War, many another battle.
Not until the biggest wars, and their economic aftermath, did things change.
Modern Ag meant more production, the old ways went by the bye, until
Mrs. Thatcher and the Common Market really did them in: these old sweet swards,
and so much else. Now everything must pay for itself, and to hell with the cowslips,
the orchids. Farmers, flowers' friends forever, forced into modern harness and sprays.
The losses epic, almost every acre gone to oilseed rape, arable, and "improved" grass,
as Audis, speeding down the lanes to save seconds on their commute, hazard
the stately pace of tractors and Travelers' vans.

Oh, I know my pastoralism is sentimental, impractical, as archaic as the Gypsies.
But I put it to you: my conservatism is deeper than Mrs. Thatcher ever visioned.
For "conservative" and "conservation" share the same root, and both *should* mean
to save the best of what's left.

Did you think this would be an elegy? Far from it. What thrilled *me*
is that *this* meadow persists. And the Romany campfire smoke in the hedge.
And farmers who still care about more than the bottom line,
though the bottom line must balance if there are still to be farms.
For when it all goes down, as Butler and Jeffries and Orwell all told us
it will, and as we know even better now if we are paying any attention at all,
this will still be here: the scraps of old grasslands, the Travelers tucked

in the hedges, the tillers who would love to return to a simpler way. All these, which may give Albion, and all the rest, a better shot next time around.

The Black Rabbit

It's not often I see six a.m. with my eyelids open.
But the cat, usually content to sleep at least as late as I,
wakes early, wants out. Downstairs, standing
at the kitchen sink, munching a bowl of granola,
thinking of going back to bed again, I see
a large black object out on the driveway
in the dawning light: beautiful, ebony, sleek,
long soft ears. Surely the cat. But wait. The cat
doesn't have long black ears. And then I see
the cat, and he is watching too.

The rabbits of *Watership Down* sometimes see
the Black Rabbit of Inlé, when one of them is about to die.
Sort of a Grim Reaper for talking leporids.
But rabbits, on the whole, cannot
actually talk. And I've seen the likes of this one
at the County Fair. Even so:
maybe I will call it Blackie the Bunny,
instead of the Black Rabbit. And maybe
I won't go back to bed right now, after all.

Elevating Animals

The dream left nothing but this phrase in my mind: "elevating animals."
I didn't know what it meant, but I knew it was right.
We should elevate the animals.

They've spent too long on the bottom rungs, exploitation, extinction, all that.
When did an animal ever get the same consideration as we give ourselves, or our self?
Thoreau said "we are conscious of an animal in us," but most of us are not. Most
are unwilling to admit that we are animals also. Okay, have it that way. Then,
we ought to elevate the animals. After all, Darwin didn't call it "The Ascent of Man,"
but "The Descent of Man." Take it as you will. But elevate the animals.

Like the rare little spotted skunk that walked into my studio last week
and, thank the gods, did not spray. Thumped a while beneath a bookcase, then sashayed
on out again into the night. But even if it had "thrown scent" (as zoologists say),
that kitten-sized civet cat (as trappers call it) made my day with its beautiful
appearance, deserves every honor I can think to give it.
We ought to elevate the animals.

Or that jumping spider basking on an iron wheel by a Missoula millpond,
with its golden flecks and its eight eyes all focused on me, forelegs lifted like paws
in warning or greeting: how easy to flick her into the water, how much better to watch
her little leaps and scampers and listen for her imprecations all that long afternoon?

Or the band-tailed pigeons exploding back and forth across my bedroom window
this morning, seventy, a hundred of them, oak to tall oak, stuffing acorns, watching
for the Cooper's hawk, sounding like a downpour, a fusillade of pearly wings,
every time they erupt from the foliage.

Oh, yes: we should elevate the animals.
For who else will ever elevate us, as they do?

September Song

Painted Lady on Buddleia in the morning,
Woodland Skippers on goldenrod. Yestereve
the air smelled of blackberry pie in the last sun.
Raiding the late surprise of berries, I put up
a cabbage white, gone to roost in the hedge.
Took two turns around my head, then settled
like a flake of parchment
against a bleached-out Marah leaf.
My friend said: I will imagine reading this
as I roll out a crust for your late-season pie.
You can picture the butterfly vents I will make
to allow the fragrant steam to escape.

The Troopers of State Route Four

I.

Driving home from Astoria, late at night. Pulled east
onto the Four in Naselle. One set of lights came up behind.
Passing lane, Salme Hill, drew alongside. Saw he was a trooper.
Slowed for him to pass, but he stayed right with me, slowed
almost to a standstill at my left, so I did the same: what's
the deal? I thought I was legal, but still you wonder. That's when
I saw the big cow elk in both our lanes just yards away.
I hadn't seen them, but he had, and saved us. I followed
him at a couple hundred yards after that, all the way
over Deep River, past Rosburg, through Gray's River,
all the way to my road. Signaled my turn, and only then
did his lights come on—just the yellows—in a brief salute
before he disappeared around the bend. In the depths
of the dark night, we'll gladly take the companions
we are offered.

II.

Roadkill by the river is always bad. You hope it's a nutria
(not native at least) or maybe a big black rat. You hope
it's not a mink, or a muskrat, or a beaver. Or worse, an otter.
But it was. The biggest dog otter I'd ever seen, right along
the center line. More than a yard from nose to pointy tail-tip,
maybe thirty pounds. Extravagant brown pelt unblemished.
I had to go back to park, walk a ways to get to it. Traffic bad,
shoulders narrow—couldn't see how I would safely do it.
And just then came the trooper. He hit

his lights, all of them this time. Cars and log trucks
stopped. I gave him a thumbs up and dove for the otter.
I could barely heft him over the guardrail and fling him,
with one arm, down the bank to the waterside. What a thud
he made, before lying there as if sleeping in the grass. I knew
better than to throw him into the water, recalling how angry
the ravens were when I'd thrown a fresh mink into the drink.
"Thanks," I said, "you came along at the perfect time."
"You bet," said the trooper, "good work." Then he killed
the blue and the red and led his little parade
on down the highway.

Drug of Choice

I was having a couple of teeth pulled out—
long roots, lower jaw, wasn't looking forward.
The laughing gas was kicking in, but not all that much.
The surgeon was having a hard time with the first tooth.
It just didn't want to come. "That's a tough one,"
he said, when he took a break. "That's why they send
them to me. Well, at least they keep my wife in shoes."
I was in no condition to reply, but my eyebrows shot up.
"My wife teaches kindergarten," he said, "and she likes
to teach in high heels. Her teacher friends think she's nuts,
but the kids just love her for it: the sparkly ones, the pink—
they love them all."
After that, the pliers were barely there.

Verlaine and Rimbaud preferred absinthe.
Coleridge opium, Shelley laudanum,
Ginsberg peyote and LSD. I just find
a good story, or an idea for a poem,
a better distraction from dental work
than all the nitrous oxide in the tank.
And, you know?
That next tooth came out eeeeasy.

Picking Blueberries

(after an August rain)

The rain came in the night, a percussive blanket
I pulled around my shoulders and into my dreams.
So the morning broke uncommonly fresh,
drops glinting off the butterfly bush like disco balls.
The blueberry leaves were wet, the big fat berries pale
with that frosty-white thing they do, over the inky blue.
I don't know what could feel as good
as reaching fingers through those cool damp leaves
to squeeze and pluck the swollen fruit, imagining
its indigo burst in my mouth, on hot oatmeal,
as the morning warms and glows,
after an August rain.

Another One Bites the Dust

Kitty was in such repose. The way he sits
beside me on the porch in the early evening,
his paws tucked beneath his chest, so pretty.
It all happened so fast. Up he leapt, sprang
down into the tall grass. A loud high "squeek,"
a double rustle in the fescue. Then he was back
again, playing rugby on the floorboards
with the biggest vole you ever saw—
short tail, broad head, altogether as big as a brat—
Microtus townsendii,
the base of this whole valley's food chain.
At least it died soon. Crunch, crunch, it went down,
except for a neat pile of giblets and the whiskered mask.
Now Kitty returns to his repose. So pretty.

The Naturalist Gets Fed Up with Nature

"the beasts of the field shall be at peace with thee"

—Job 5:23

Was it strictly necessary for the lovely doe and her spotty fawns
to eat ALL of the flowerbuds on my phlox?
Or the thrushes: did they need every one of the red currants?
You bees in my wall—I know I've encouraged you
and built you little yellow porches; but did your last two swarms
really have to take place IN my living room?
And yes, I am fond of the big brown bats
that visit the bedroom many nights.
But must their near-face fly-bys always come around three a.m.
during really good dreams?
Plus, I'm not sure that the thousands of flying ants that emerged
in my studio last week were entirely sanctioned.
The deer mice that plug the auto's heater again and again,
the packrats with their bushels of missing objects,
the slugs that slide in on the kitchen floor,
the long-legged spiders that catch the flies, oh yes,
but then crap all over my books—
and that's just the fauna so far!
O creatures, creatures, creatures . . . how you occupy my life.

What would I do without you?

Pursuit of the Lady

She lays her coral petticoats out flat beside her
taking in the last of the late coral sun
her every movement is voluptuous
she is a voluptuary to the last minutes of the sun
her exquisite senses twitch to her surroundings
she is exquisitely vulnerable. Hasn't yet seen
her suitor. Oleaginous, he stalks her,
as he has for some time now.
Sometimes she almost feels it
(his greedy eyes on her soft downy back
his soft mouth parted for her flesh)
but so far he's hidden his obsession
obsessed with her as he is, engrossed
by her little twitches, his gross passions.
His lust contends with her determination
toward the sun, his own determined trigger to pounce.
Can he help himself? He cannot. His purpose
brooks no reason, needs no help from anyone
but maybe patience. She is anything but patient.
Ladylike, she pulls in her coral petticoats
extends her downy, spring-like legs
just as he springs for her once more,
and once more finds her gone. Her fate,
if a second slower, easy to imagine from that
of the slower moths, which he eats on my
lamp-lit bed on summer nights.

(*Vanessa cardui* [painted lady butterfly] and *Felis catus*)

Stepping on Snails

Fool: "Cans't tell how an oyster makes its shell?"
Lear: "No."
Fool: "Nor I neither; but I can tell why a snail has his house."
Lear: "Why?"
Fool: "Why, to put's head in; not to . . . leave his horns without a case."

—William Shakespeare, King Lear I:5

It happens sometimes in the garden at night
if I come back indoors without a light:
that sickening crackle that means my foot's found
some elegant home, some snail carried 'round.

Some broken-shelled snails can be repaired
but it's not in the cards if their bodies are bared.
The merciful thing would be long-snouted beetle
or sweet-talking thrush between warble and wheedle.

It's not just the wreck of that beautiful swirl,
the keenest desire of my boyhood world,
nor taking the luckless mollusk's life—
unaware, we assume, of love, or strife.

What troubles me are the ones that *don't* die,
their castles shattered in bits where they lie.
And what I'd like to ask, of the snails I've tread on,
is what does night weigh, when you meet it head on?

Library of Libraries

He and I were talking about our personal libraries. How we had assembled
them and cared for them and played with them and loved them,
and, what the hell are we going to do with them, anyway?

This isn't a rare thing for readers. Whether on a single shelf or in their own annex,
we gather our printed goods and celebrate them with every sense. They give
us so much pleasure, we feel they deserve a future beyond us, all together.

But who will care? Who will read them, keep them, feel and smell and dust them,
take them down and put them back in just the proper place? Who, indeed,
as I did for my parents' books, and some of my grandmother's hundreds.

No one, that's who, unless you're one of the lucky few with a bookworm kid.
It'll be Goodwill, or bulk rate with a used book dealer, or pulp, at worst.
I guess that's why I had the dream, out of desperation.

In the dream was a great big building with many rooms—a one-time school,
or institution, or factory. Each room had a name on the door, and inside,
all the books that person owned: shelved just as they'd been at home,
no Dewey Decimal System or Library of Congress numbers here.

It was a library of libraries! And when you went inside, you would see
not only *all those books*, but what made each book-lover tick: each room
a biography in books. Lots of chairs, and desks, and day-beds—you could stay
for the day, for the night, for a week, or forever.

We could do it! There are lots of empty buildings. We just need a few grand—
and a truck.

Leaves

November sun brings breezes off the river,
out of the valley, from every compass point,
tweaking leaves from black walnuts and beeches.
Their butterfly flight flickers every which way,
till they settle onto the spackled grass.
Then another gust comes up
neither easterly nor west
but somehow 360, like a geyser of air
from right out of the ground,
stirring every bright leaf into play.
Suddenly the entire sky is filled
with gold and copper spinners
all sparkling in the autumn sun,
a treasure chest emptied in unquiet seas.
The whole field of vision *scintillates*
into my retinas, into my memory forever.

So when I learn a little later
(as people do these days)
that my dad of seventy-two years
was not my actual father
I have a beautiful picture handy
with which to blot it out.

The Waning of the Worm Moon

They call it the Worm Moon because earthworms come out
this time of year, beginning their vernal perambulation
over the lawns and fields and under the roots of things.

This March moon, known too as Crow Moon, Crust Moon,
Chaste Moon, Sugar Moon, and Sap Moon, for the maples.
But should the moon care what we call it? Happy
just to direct the worms, just to beguile us
into stepping outside on a chilly night to gaze
on it, to poke about the silvered edges of the turf,
to see if it is true: will the worms come out tonight?

But then it goes past, this fullness. The Worm Moon
becomes just another nameless, gibbous glob, melting
into the night-time sky, sliding toward its nullity.
And we, who thought we were special
for seeing it, for knowing its name, go back
to normalcy: just people, waiting for the worms.

How Dare You?

Standing at the corner
its top like a little capitol dome
with a five-sided nut for a lantern.
Below, the stubby tower planted in the ground
spigots on either side for hoses,
a bigger one in front, where
the tanker might hook on.
Running around the rim, the raised motto:
"WH Fittings and Valves
Anniston, Alabama: 1965"
the whole of it freshly painted
In bright, canary yellow.

Who would dare to write of daffodils these days
(like Wordsworth, like Larkin)
when missiles fall on Kyiv
and glaciers are on the melt everywhere?
I do, because Mike, on the corner,
planted six daffodils in a clump
beside the hydrant in his yard.
They are blooming now, along with one
random dandelion, all the same yellow as the fire plug,

and in the late afternoon sun, they blaze.

This Kind of Place

At the end of my mail walk, the box
lies bang in the wet grass. Rats,
somebody's bumped it. But, no—
the mail lady says it came away in her hands,
the post rotted off flush at the ground.

Sad to see that big brown tube laid low.
Bought it new and shiny, nailed it down, sank
the post in the valley turf that very first fall.
Forty years it's rusted there, keeping
all that mail sound and dry, ever upright.

Five-mile drive for the mail with it down,
then a big job to fix it in cold wet rain.
So when I come back,
with pipe and strap and sledge, I *gasp*
to see my mailbox UP again, soundly braced
with green wire and two green fence posts.

How did it get that way? I have no idea, maybe
never will. It's just the kind of place
where such a thing can happen.

ACKNOWLEDGMENTS & PUBLICATION CREDITS

The poems in this book are for the most part new and uncollected. A number of them have appeared in the following publications, whose permission to reprint is gratefully acknowledged:

The Tidewater Reach: A Field Guide to the Lower Columbia in Poems and Pictures (Longview, WA: Columbia River Reader Press); *Butterfly Launches from Spar Pole* (CD, vinyl LP, and streaming album, with Krist Novoselic and Ray Prestegard, Murky Slough Music); *An Island in the Stream: Ecocritical and Literary Responses to Cuban Environmental Culture* (Washington, DC: Lexington Books); *The Evolution of the Genus* Iris and *Chinook & Chanterelle* (Liberty Lake, WA: Lost Horse Press); *Children of the Night* (chapbook), (Gray's River, WA: New Riverside Press); *Camas*; *Coast Weekend* (Astoria, OR); *Columbia River Reader*; *Hipfish*; *North Coast Squid*; *Rain*; *Salal*; *Upper Left Edge*; *Wahkiakum County Eagle*; *The Warbler*.

My warm thanks go to all the poets of Ric's Poetry Mic in Astoria, Oregon, first responders to many of these poems, especially Florence Sage, Jim Dott, John Ciminello, and Jennifer Nightingale. As always, to my faithful and long-time supporters JoAnne Heron, Fayette Krause, David Branch, Neil Johannsen, Krist Novoselic, and Christine Holbert. And to my many poet friends: you make my words better with yours.

At Texas Tech University Press and the Sowell Collection, I sincerely thank Travis Snyder, Christie Perlmutter, Hannah Gaskamp, Dina López, John Brock, Diane Warner, Kurt Caswell, and Kristin Loyd, and everyone else who helped to bring this book into being.

Most of all, deepest thanks from my very heart to the poet Florence Sage, best sweetheart, friend, critic, and poetry pal a fella could have: *sine qua non*.

Finally, this, for Neil Johannsen, for his wonderful cover painting:

Once Upon a Bear

Guy walks into my little nook in Anderson Hall, sits down at the desk
opposite mine. Afternoon light falls through mullioned windows
of the forestry school, onto his handsome Nordic face.
"I guess we're office mates," he says. That was Neil, at the start.

Fast forward half a century
past beers at the Viking, field trips to the Hoh, shooting stars
purpling green spring hills of the Gold Country for his wedding.
Past families and jobs, cats and vans, hikes and paddles.

Past many a meal at table or campsite or pub, past
any number of birds and books and beers—
till now, two ancient friends connected by the mail,
hunkered in our rural holts a few hours of road apart.

Birds and beers, you bet. But now I needed a bear. Once
a lad on horseback from a ranch in Petaluma, turned ranger
then big parks-boss, now a painter of cormorants and cats—
could Neil paint me a bear?

In short, he did— the perfect bear, a crazy rainbow bear,
Bob's Bear—to grace the cover of this book. But it came at a cost.
Sketch after sketch the artist made, not his usual way. Then
start after start at the paint laid down, no, not his M.O. at all.

Went on for weeks, enough to drive any artist bats.
But it was my bear, and it had to be right.
I told him writers face the heavy hand of editors too.
Cold comfort, when you're the one being stifled.

Then he painted one more bear: the bear no one expected,
least of all himself, and everyone who saw it knew,
and maybe even the bear itself—
it was the perfect bear
for the book. And we all said, that's that.

Two old guys with all that beer between us, and now, a bear:
Just look!

ABOUT THE AUTHOR

Robert Michael Pyle is the author of twenty-eight books of essays, natural history, fiction, and poems, including a flight of well-known butterfly books. His previous poetry collections are *Evolution of the Genus* Iris, *Chinook & Chanterelle*, and *The Tidewater Reach*. He is a John Burroughs Medalist (*Wintergreen*) and a Guggenheim Fellow (*Where Bigfoot Walks*), among many other literary and conservation awards. A Yale-trained ecologist and Honorary Life Fellow of both the Royal and American Entomological Societies, he founded the renowned Xerces Society for Invertebrate Conservation. Bob Pyle has dwelled along a rural tributary of the Lower Columbia River for forty-five years, along with the jays, the band-tailed pigeons, and the voles.

AUTHOR PHOTO BY THEA LINNAEA PYLE